Bridge of Words

Thérèse Corfiatis
and Britta Stenberg

Bridge of Words

For Dr Thomas William (Tom) Langston OAM
16/4/1950–14/4/2020
Choirmaster, teacher, musician who devoted his life to music and the community. He believed music to be vital in developing social capital and strengthening connections. In Tom's words, 'I didn't choose music, music chose me.'

Bridge of Words
ISBN 978 1 76109 362 3
Copyright © Thérèse Corfiatis and Britta Stenberg 2022
Cover image: original art by Britta Stenberg

First published 2022 by
Ginninderra Press
PO Box 3461 Port Adelaide 5015
www.ginninderrapress.com.au

Contents

Unaffected	Britta Stenberg	7
The Tiniest Moment	Britta Stenberg	8
Music of Water Sweden	Britta Stenberg	9
Music of Water Tasmania	Thérèse Corfiatis	10
Birds in Winter Rain	Thérèse Corfiatis	11
Reflections on Covid-19	Thérèse Corfiatis	12
Reflections on Lockdown	Britta Stenberg	13
April	Britta Stenberg	14
Summer Rain in July	Britta Stenberg	15
Winter Rain and Horses in July	Thérèse Corfiatis	16
To a Sparky, in Winter	Thérèse Corfiatis	17
Water and Grief	Britta Stenberg	18
The Midnight Sun	Britta Stenberg	19
A Bridge Between Hemispheres	Thérèse Corfiatis	20
The Wind Sent Me a Leaf	Britta Stenberg	21
On This Fine Morning	Thérèse Corfiatis	23
In Memory of My Mother's Birthday	Thérèse Corfiatis	24
In Memory of a Summer Spoken	Britta Stenberg	26
Meeting With an Old Woman	Britta Stenberg	27
Before Leaving	Britta Stenberg	29
End of Season	Britta Stenberg	30
Words with Wings	Britta Stenberg	31
In Memory of Björn	Britta Stenberg	32
Missing Tom	Britta Stenberg	33
The Autumn Leaf	Britta Stenberg	34
Little Bird	Thérèse Corfiatis	35
A Memory of Cascade Gardens	Thérèse Corfiatis	37
Autumn Cries Out	Britta Stenberg	38
Horse in Rain	Thérèse Corfiatis	39
Upon the Living Air	Thérèse Corfiatis	40

Horses	Britta Stenberg	42
A Teardrop of Rain	Britta Stenberg	43
Night Manoeuvres	Thérèse Corfiatis	44
Spring Twilight Over Ocean	Thérèse Corfiatis	45
Everywhere the Green Fell Down	Thérèse Corfiatis	46
Let Me Stay	Britta Stenberg	47
In a Star-filled Night	Britta Stenberg	48
Light and Gum Trees	Thérèse Corfiatis	49
Beings of Two Worlds	Thérèse Corfiatis	50
My Mother's Sewing Basket	Thérèse Corfiatis	52
Late Afternoon Low Tide	Thérèse Corfiatis	52
Oppression	Thérèse Corfiatis	54
In My Studio	Britta Stenberg	55
Friendship	Thérèse Corfiatis	56
Everyone Needs a Dream	Thérèse Corfiatis	57
My Dreams	Britta Stenberg	58
Christmas Flowers for Britta	Thérèse Corfiatis	59
Under a Full Moon	Britta Stenberg	60
Song for Tom	Thérèse Corfiatis	61
Shadow Self	Thérèse Corfiatis	62
Star Paths	Thérèse Corfiatis	63
Footprints in the Snow	Britta Stenberg	64
Days	Thérèse Corfiatis	65
Frogs	Thérèse Corfiatis	66
Cat	Thérèse Corfiatis	67
In Praise of Summer	Thérèse Corfiatis	68
Bird Haiku	Thérèse Corfiatis	69
Good Friday Full Moon	Thérèse Corfiatis	70
Peach Haiku	Thérèse Corfiatis	72
Retrospective	Britta Stenberg	73
Seagull Variations	Thérèse Corfiatis	74
Sing a Song Just for Me	Britta Stenberg	75
Visit to a Nursing Home	Thérèse Corfiatis	76

Unaffected

As a stone in the middle of a stream
I listen to the world
above my head –
birds sing unaffected

Britta Stenberg

The Tiniest Moment

Under my shoe, gravel rattles
as thought
blending with light and vulnerability
awaits tomorrow

Britta Stenberg

Music of Water   Sweden

In the silence
ice slowly melts
dripping
breaking apart
while the river
prepares its song

Newborn freedom
accompanies singing birds
the river's symphony
a free spirit
untouched by human hands

Bass notes vibrate
until the ground trembles
this force pours out its power
navigating cliffs and rocks
life streaming
within the river's symphony

Britta Stenberg

Music of Water   Tasmania

Heard high upon the hill
music of water
drifts up from the ocean
a crooning heart
constantly moving
never still

Music of water
splashes to the shore
tides rise and fall
embryonic memories
lift up, resurface
the heart remembers all

Thérèse Corfiatis

Birds in Winter Rain

Crumbs scattered for the birds
they descend in waves
from wet trees

fluttering wings cast off droplets
crystal orbs
held in jewelled light

Thérèse Corfiatis

Reflections on Covid-19

as when small
things that comfort
comfort still

clouds puffed full
light-tossed sea
sunshine on the windowsill

cat curled in sleep
birds in choir
rose scent permeating air

wind in trees
as shadows play
imagination running there

love of family
love of friends
steadfast things that never end

as when small
things that comfort
comfort still

Thérèse Corfiatis

Reflections on Lockdown

One breath from death
the experts say
four newborn kittens in the box
my windows need cleaning

Keeping distance
is all that matters
I turn my face
towards the rising sun

New reports of deaths
no one is safe any more
the kitten's fur
is soft against my cheek

Trees are budding
as if nothing's happened
writing letters
I should have done before

One breath from death
the experts say
I make ready the season's plants
hoping they shall grow

Britta Stenberg

April

Long shadows
lay themselves upon the snow
weightless
softly on its surface

Spring comes fast
people go outside
in layers of clothing
seeking sun

Sitting in the snow
they make coffee on an open fire
as we always do
this time of year

Melting snow
drips away over time
darkness gone
sets us free

Shadows live again
without the sun
we couldn't see them
at all

Britta Stenberg

Summer Rain in July

Grey sky
hiding sun
raindrops falling
to earth

A baby is born

No fear
no darkness
anymore

Rain washes
cleansing all

Heavy drops like tears
of happiness
makes life grow

Summer light is here
to stay

A baby is born

Britta Stenberg

Winter Rain and Horses in July

From the hill high above
wet paddocks shimmer
sheets of water, in patches
tiny lakes, still and bright.

Horses gallop along fence-lines
manes and tails streaming
banners of kinship
coats rippling in light.

One stops to play
hooves splashing water
like a child jumping puddles
such happy delight.

Our joy becomes fused
joined together in time,
the smallest of moments
most sublime.

Thérèse Corfiatis

To a Sparky, in Winter

An earnest face,
he came with van and accoutrements
and as he worked
fingers deft and certain
we talked of this
and talked of that

Covid-19
Elon Musk's satellites in space
climate change

The Governor General's 1975 sacking
of Prime Minister Gough Whitlam,
archives recently made public

Feral cats decimating Tasmanian wildlife

And I thought
how aware, how bright this man
shining his light
speaking his truth
rising early in winter's chill
to earn bread for his family

We can't live on Mars, he said
we've only got this planet to call our home
Amen, I thought   Amen

Save us from our own inaction

Thérèse Corfiatis

Water and Grief

He is here now
the plumber
His name is Jim

He is going to fix our water
Everybody needs water
he says
Without water you are lost

His father disappeared last year
was never found
He grieves
He has a lot of unanswered questions
in him

He takes his tools
down to the basement
to fix the water for me
His shoulders are bent, his hair is grey
He carries all his questions within him

How could his father disappear
just like that
Without a trace?

Jim doesn't know
no one does
But he fixed my water
so I can survive

Britta Stenberg

The Midnight Sun

I'm travelling
through a tunnel
of trees
fir, pine and birch
all green
many sorts of green
I can see their differences
standing like priests
in silent prayer
I long for this moment
to last a lifetime
the road seems infinite to me
On the horizon
a blue mountain shines
in the light of the midnight sun
I'm driving through this tunnel of forest
and I can hear
trees whispering
understanding my solitude
even they have felt the burden
of a never-ending winter

The sun and me
It's us now

Britta Stenberg

A Bridge Between Hemispheres

It amazes me
how fellow travellers on this earth
meet, almost by accident –
a circumstance not unusual

For me, a friendship born
from a long-distance introduction –
two women unknown to each other,
one in the northern hemisphere
one in the southern hemisphere,
joined by the man
who knew them both

He, a creator of music and song
they, writers of words
discovering commonalities
a purposeful bridge of connection

Sudden death stole him
from their lives
but his original intention
to join these two women
lives on beyond death
lays itself down
upon the sweet altar of friendship

Two women
crossing hemispheres with their words
in the shadow of his soaring wings

Thérèse Corfiatis

The Wind Sent Me a Leaf

The wind sent me a leaf
from a foreign tree
a closer look
revealed
there was no difference
no difference at all

I too was a leaf
twirling around
trying to find
new meanings
true narratives
about life's lessons

we were the same, he and I
separated by distance
but we are both leaves
sharing similarities and differences
from the tree
we fell from

All those energies
emanating from us
so much still to be done
so much held within us
about who we are as human beings
reaching out to each other

Before he left
he gave me someone new
to keep on doing
what is yet undone
another spirit to share life's journey
and its quest for meaning

We build bridges
although we are just leaves
dancing on the wind
peering into each other's souls
there is no difference between us
no difference at all

Britta Stenberg

On This Fine Morning

On this fine morning
whatever God looks down on me
my heart is full

I feel a love so fierce
my bones are singing
every breath a ringing exhortation

I feel a sacred pull
in all that lives and grows and moves
the swaying tree, the sea, the arc of sun

I feel a holiness so deep
it permeates each cell and sanctifies
the light, the air, soft kiss of wind

On this fine morning
I ask for nothing, just to 'be'
in preparation, eyes wide open, for immortality

Thérèse Corfiatis

In Memory of My Mother's Birthday

7/8/20

This day so blue –
sky a temple of brilliant arching light

We placed spring flowers by her plaque
tender words spoken
for ourselves
for those who loved her
and could not be here

And then, a long silence
caught up in webs of inner thought
memories and images
spinning comfort in our hearts

Later, we drove winding country roads
landscape moving like a dream
a place she loved with all her being –
farms lifting up and disappearing into earth's folds
chocolate soil all sown in rows
snow-capped bluff and hills beyond
all things vibrating like a living song

Our hearts were full –
he, for a wife
I, for my mother
gratitude winging on the air
immeasurable beyond compare

And as I sat and stared out upon the world
she rose up in me like a radiating sun
our breath and bone and gristle fused as one

Thérèse Corfiatis

In Memory of a Summer Spoken

Mist covers the glittering water
like a silence
holding memories of the past

Summer ends in white wings
above my head
hiding mountains and the green valley
in a soft touch, like love

Flowers are preparing
for their long sleep
mist moves closer
singing farewell songs
we know from before

Berries are deep red now
ready for picking
treasures for winter

The smell of clean air
deep breaths inhaled
while behind the hovering mist
everything is in readiness
a comfort to me

Britta Stenberg

Meeting With an Old Woman

Japan

We met with a smile
a short shimmering moment
she recited stories from the past

her eyes have seen the blackest of days
and faced death –
even so, she still smiles

A disaster, a terrible storm
fell upon her and her family
a poison, the evil of destruction

She smiled as she told me
how life gives and takes
how mankind cannot comprehend such things

In Hiroshima's memorial house
a three-wheeled bicycle stands alone
never to be used again

Shoes left behind, bags, keys
like ghosts
leaving shadows on the wall

Photos of people running
reveal her
in that fleeing crowd

The woman that I met
with dark glittering eyes
hair in traditional style

Her hands pressed together
a gesture of bowing
of humbleness

At the centre of a burning inferno –
she tells me
now she can forgive

Her history burned
into my bones
left white scars on my skin

Forever reminding me
of the madness
of nuclear bombs

Britta Stenberg

Before Leaving

before leaving
single bird on the ground
will be left behind

Britta Stenberg

End of Season

end of season
birds are picking last corn
before going

Britta Stenberg

Words with Wings

A world of words
like rain falling on my head
like shimmering moonlight
which can be seen on our planet
wherever we may be

A world of words
spread by the wind
powerful words
friendly words
touching my cheek

I am standing in light
surrounded
by all kinds of words
I am listening

In between
the short silences
there are songs
coming from many voices

Healing songs
from every nation

Britta Stenberg

In Memory of Björn

I said, 'Go!'
only that one time,
but lots of times I said, 'Stay!'

As you slowly moved away from me
like a ship into the fog
I could barely see your wake
in the calm dark water

I was busy that evening, as always
doing nothing special

An island of pain hides the ship
as you sailed away

The room seems empty
without your dreadful pipe smoke
without your beautiful laughter
without arguments over silly things
that I can't remember any more

I am the walls
I am the room
I walk through the door, breath the air
missing the smoke in it

I wait for one glimmering star to fall
Just one star

Britta Stenberg

Missing Tom

I can't hear any notes,
it's so quiet
raindrops fall softly to earth
the cathedral door is closed
only shadows remain

I hesitate,
then take the handle of the heavy door
it opens a little,
a river of light flows out

It was here
in this cathedral of friendship
you existed for a moment
and always

Here inside
your memory dances
carried by your song
Here inside, is the sound of your voice
and joy

Here inside
there is a power
stronger than this deep sorrow
larger than this painful loss

I look around and say, 'Thanks Tom'
thank you for owning this huge space
and for letting us into it

Britta Stenberg

The Autumn Leaf

The forest is burning with colour

Leaves know how
ahead of time, to fall
upon the ground

One,
just a single one
is left
red and yellow, and shining

If you listen carefully
you can hear it singing

> I have faith
> I have strength
> I never hesitate

I know the winter is coming
but I won't leave my place
I'm going to stay here and watch
everyone of you

Britta Stenberg

Little Bird

for Monica

She came into my life
like a wounded little bird
a twisted ankle forcing her
to rethink life's direction

And so
this woman with a little bird
tattooed on her shoulder
found the courage to sing again
and grew to understand
how those dwelling in dark, deep shadows
drained her vital essences, energies and sleep

within the sheltered spaces
of her inner core
she found a place to perch
watching the world with bright eyes
safe inside her leafy kingdom

in the green garden
little birds flitted like jewels
amongst sighing trees
instilling joy and wonder

her wounded heart healed
as she burnt written words
set down in a ceramic bowl, at dusk
paper curling like tiny tongues
smoke rising in an offering to the sky

new hopes raised themselves up
ashes scattering (like little birds)
taking flight upon the wind –
how sweetly the universe reveals its truths

she and I would sit
basking in each other's smiles

affection warming our souls with soft feathery hands
the roots of our tree nourished
our leaves glistening in light –
a place for us to grow and thrive

my little bird and me

Thérèse Corfiatis

A Memory of Cascade Gardens

South Hobart

Autumn sun is warming
clouds skittering high
sounds of children
playing in the schoolyard
drift up the hill
clear and bright, upon the wind

Thoughts stir
of childhood autumn mornings
chilled fingers, toes
when cold cheeks felt like fire,
fond memories drift like leaves
of the Gardens near my home

Trees, russet and gold
spread embracing arms
such beauty there adorning greenest lawns
a time when nature soothed
an anxious heart
a lesson learnt which still remains

Declare your pact with beauty
carry it wherever you go
all this and more, remembered
as children's voices
drift up the hill
clear and bright, upon the wind

Thérèse Corfiatis

Autumn Cries Out

I have never thought of autumn
as my best friend

I cannot feel the sadness
I knew before
I just hear its voice
crying out
in strong colours

Smells of ripe apples
birds singing farewell songs
all has my name on it

In spring, my mind was busy
I did not hear

In summer there was only a whisper
I strained to hear

But now in autumn
it is obvious
I have learned to recognise
life as it really is

As autumn makes its offering
I humbly receive the gift

Britta Stenberg

Horse in Rain

They stand in pairs
their inner sides
fending off wind and rain –
outer flanks running in rivulets

Even so, as water gathers
around them in shining sheets
necks are bent, intent
on munching grassy delights

The horses seem content
sure of themselves
stock still within a wet whirling world
bodies strong enough to endure

Thérèse Corfiatis

Upon the Living Air

Beneath a grey dome of cloudy layered sky
high above a bowl of barely moving sea
rain gently eased away –
a quiet hush of early morning resting there

The scene before me
looked as if outstretched hands trailing water
had swept across the land
and left behind a soft palette of glistening dampness –
silence broken only by bird call
within still-dripping trees

Praise given for this deep and sacred peace
a reverent benediction laid down
upon the heads of tall stooped gums
(leaves clustered, in bunches, like small knuckled fists)
laid down upon the spears of bottlebrush
where gold and vermilion wands lift up
vibrant splashes against duller greens

The gleam, the sheen of frail new grass
the flash of wings, birds speeding by
all held beneath this morning sky
all held within the soul and eye
atumbling down the hills
of gorse and springtime daffodils
native trees and plants
refuge for pademelons, bandicoots and snakes
of marching insects, feral cats

Birds feeding on the bottlebrush
heads bobbing into honeyed-yellow depths
then bobbing into bolder reds
flowers bright
against dark feathered heads

This scene of perfect beauty
drawn in with every breath
a mystical potion upon the living air
enough to last, endure forever
in the beholder's heart

Thérèse Corfiatis

Horses

In my childhood
we had a horse named 'Star'.
She lived in her small stable
and we fed her
hay from last summer,
covered her with blankets
to protect her from severe cold.
We caressed her
and held her to a promise of hard work
in the woods.
This was her life.
She blinked slowly
as if she understood.
No one could work outside
in minus 30 degrees.
She was a clever girl,
our Star.

Britta Stenberg

A Teardrop of Rain

A teardrop of rain
falls into my open hand.
The old tree
naked and alone
Wants my attention.
I hold, I watch
a shimmering drop
just for me to see,
a single drop
bequeathing important stories
as tears always do.

Britta Stenberg

Night Manoeuvres

for Alexander

We played all afternoon
his laughter light and full –
he sang songs of his own devising
words not quite formed
done sweetly though
in notes that rose and fell
behind a perfect curving mouth
teeth like tiny pearls

Evening fell, grey with rain
I took him to his bed –
awriggling, ajiggling
he fought impending sleep
cuddles and lullabies soothing
his breath created its own rhythm
until tiredness overtook him

A kiss upon his soft brow
I slipped quietly out his door
and left for home
my heart so stored with love
it carried me into the midnight hour
and lay down with me
beneath a starry sky

Thérèse Corfiatis

Spring Twilight Over Ocean

A pale spring evening
a gathering mistiness
hovers upon horizons
light fading
blue-silver tones

Shape and movement swirl
a gentle vibrancy
as if to say
day is ending
all is well with the world

Air is fresh, salty
a tang speaking to the life
of deepest seas
while clouds above
lay out their prayers
in folded hands

Thérèse Corfiatis

Everywhere the Green Fell Down

Everywhere the green fell down
it filled my heart
with its silent sound
green all around

It moved and spoke
in flowers and bees
and thrusting growth
of fields and trees

It held the light
amidst branches green
poplars tall beside the road
risen up like emerald flames

I felt such joy
in its silent sound
as everywhere the green fell down
green all around

Thérèse Corfiatis

Let Me Stay

In this moment
I look for a flower
where none are, any more
just there, in my mind
my green fantasy
countless roses still give me
their best memories,
my life goes on
day by day
light shortens
like time, fading away
thank you for being there
helping my mind open
so I can hear the breeze
from whispering trees
feel the warm touch
from sunshine lost to me in time,
let me stay
just one more moment
let me dream
surrounded by cold winter.

Britta Stenberg

In a Star-filled Night

Walking
on a crispy road
the air is cold
my breath exhales
like white smoke
as I look at the sky's black roof
covered with thousands and thousands of stars
I have a strong feeling
that one of them is a sign
a message from you
I see it blinking
as if you speak to me
in this moment
this quiet moment
we have an endless connection

Britta Stenberg

Light and Gum Trees

Evening light
slants across a stand of gums –
trunks sheen, an otherworldly glow
alabaster-saffron columns
rise up in beauty like a silent prayer
suffusing sacredness upon the air

Clustered treetops move gently
partners in dance
to swaying limb and branch
birds flutter into leafy sanctuaries
like puffs of feathered breath, all in a trance
interwoven upon approaching night

Thérèse Corfiatis

Beings of Two Worlds

October is the month of whale migration

I lay in bed
and imagine them
sliding beneath silvery seas
large and dark and powerful
calling to each other in song
occasionally surfacing
to gaze at the moon and starlit heavens

I wish for whales
to visit me in their dreams
to tell me their secrets
to share their journeys
to show me their little ones
and to forgive us
for what we have done to their home

Thérèse Corfiatis

My Mother's Sewing Basket

All her deftness and clever craft held within this space

tapestries toiled over for many years
ribbons, threads, needles and lace
embroideries stitched

minuscule pearls and stars
tiny metal flowers
embellishments and decorations
for felt, cotton, satin and linen
precious fabrics

elastics, pins, buttons, buckles
repair kits for carpets and upholstery
coloured threads of every hue
knitting needles, crochet hooks

an old pattern for caftans
to fend off summer sun
iron-on patches
measuring tapes, hooks and press studs

chunky old scissors
worn and sharp –
how many dresses, curtains, materials
had she cut with them?

I visualise her beautiful hands
long slender fingers, shapely nails
of how she sewed my little clothes
and tended me when small

and as she aged and became ill
her fingers, bent and twisted
held mine until the very last –
a mother's love sits with me still

Thérèse Corfiatis

Late Afternoon Low Tide

Sea unravels its shoreline –
sunlight suffuses golden hues
upon a tousled carpet of patterned rocks
and craggy inlets

Stone looks like ruffled lace
adorning sandy beaches –
pretty edges stitched tight
in little knots of purling waves

Ocean and sky
swirl and shift and murmur
spontaneous and sinuous
varying shades of majestic blue

Small tidal pools
reflect passing clouds and birds
planets and stars at night
an unending passage of images and movement

Water, of its own accord
mirrors life on earth
partner to our embryonic form
two hearts beating as one

Thérèse Corfiatis

Oppression

for Kylie Moore-Gilbert

truth can't be tortured
truth can't be hung by the neck
murdered, incarcerated, spirited away

for every man, woman or child
who fall like flowers petals
to an embracing earth

seeds of truth shall spring and bloom
beauty and brightness resurrected
stronger than before

Thérèse Corfiatis

In My Studio

4/12/2020

I am painting yellow
yearnings of desire
and I've even chosen white
although I see it everywhere
this calm, quiet whiteness

I listen to the sounds of fear
people running
without leaving their place
some of them
stay held in their own emptiness

I watch it
I listen to it
reports of new deaths every day
those figures mean nothing but fear

If I listen closely
to music from history
it creates a composition
full of green and red and yellow

I notice
I have been painting
everything in circles

Britta Stenberg

Friendship

for K. H.

we are light beings
shape shifters
wise empaths
old souls with new ideas

star sliders
sea dancers
moon gazers
dawn drifters

we are atomic neurons
soul fusion
cosmic flyers
nebulae eaters

we are stream singers
tree worshippers
energy makers
all this, and much more

Thérèse Corfiatis

Everyone Needs a Dream

for Leo

Everyone needs a dream
a place to shake away
sorrows of the heart
a place of peace and simple joys
a place where love can never be destroyed

For some
dreams come on starlit-studded skies
or ride upon the wild and hurling wind
can softly whisper within leafy trees
or water trickling over stone

Everyone needs a dream
enough to last through each and every day
restoring hope, creating cheer
enough to fill our yearning souls –
a dream to guide the way

Thérèse Corfiatis

My Dreams

Sailing on my ocean of dreams
I put on my life-jacket
in case it's needed
every now and then

I hold my finger up
checking where to go
to feel the wind
helpful ally

Sometimes days are becalmed
sometimes there's rain and thunder –
dreams feel like salt water
upon my skin

Or like being hidden in a cave
surrounded by snow and frozen ice –
the ocean of my dreams
is still my friend

Britta Stenberg

Christmas Flowers for Britta

25/12/2020

I think of her today
in Sweden's ice and snow
a frozen silent world
so different from my own.

Tasmania sparkles beneath blue summer skies
everything blooming and growing and good
I wander the garden in late afternoon
and savour the flowers, a feast for my eyes.

Red kangaroo paws on the longest of stems
golden bottlebrush feed bees and birds as they come
wild orchids, soft pink, resemble pale sunset clouds
green ferns unfold fronds, like songs without sound.

Flowers of white tea-tree like fresh ocean froth
wattle's bright yellow, eucalyptus' dull green
colours so varied, no two the same
a garden ragged, unkempt, but only in name.

They lift up their heads, in praise, so it seems
of an earth needing peace and beautiful dreams
as I write these words to my friend far away
a memory to keep of our Christmas day.

Thérèse Corfiatis

Under a Full Moon

While I watch the evening star
gleaming and twinkling yellows and reds,
I stand at the centre of everything
and I know I own the sky
as the full moon's light
spreads out from me
making sharp shadows
drawing grey shapes
on the surface of hard blue snow

A white hare
runs quickly, ears like lace

Safe in this quiet place
I am standing in this moment
my tiny fragment of the earth
and as I look about me, the full moon
is suddenly gone.

Britta Stenberg

Song for Tom

In memory of Tom Langston; memorial service held Saturday,
30/1/2021 – Ulverstone Rowing Club, Tasmania

This summer day is beaming
brighter than any other gone
sky's blue mantle shining
windswept ocean full of song

Light plays on jewelled waves
foam-tipped and shoreward bound
birds are winging, trees are singing
for you, my dear friend Tom

I hear your music everywhere
in the dance of stars at night
at dawn when all things move and stir
motes of dust upon sunlight

Wherever you journey, dearest Tom
may we meet again one day under summer skies
raise a glass to friendship and simple joys
to the light in each other's eyes

Thérèse Corfiatis

Shadow Self

My shadow self
sits in the corner
on a chair
pointing a finger at me

I look over my shoulder

No one is there

My shadow self smiles
unnerving
watching me
like a hawk

Silence cuts the air between us

I can almost hear
wings lifting up
flapping gently
as if to carry me away

Thérèse Corfiatis

Star Paths

Silver seas
in sheets of stillness
reflect the moon, our guide

Stars strung out
in points of light
a stream of clustered signs

Worlds stretched out
eternal paths
whirling without end

Places yet unknown to us
where prayers and wisdom collide
all this and more, revealed to us

Upon those timeless skies

Thérèse Corfiatis

Footprints in the Snow

for Tom

I saw footprints in the snow
left by someone unknown
they will be gone in time

There are footprints in my mind
held gently, softly
that no one can replace

What did death say
when it first visited him?
What was its message?

Did he make an agreement
that it would step aside
for a moment
wanting me to find some one
to keep his footprints safe
never to forget?

He gave us our vision
it doesn't melt away
his footprints will never be destroyed

Is this what he created
when he made his footprints permanent
for all the world to see?

Britta Stenberg

Days

days dissolve
swept away in racing cloud
dreams fade on waking

Thérèse Corfiatis

Frogs

small frogs sing
heavy rains fall unabated
songs are tiny gongs

Thérèse Corfiatis

Cat

cat scratches carpet
claws eagerly sharpened
birds strut outside

Thérèse Corfiatis

In Praise of Summer

As summer ended
light lingered in perfect azure skies
days shortened, fading like a dream –
shades of rose and peach and dusky violet

As summer ended
dragonflies whirled about the garden
armadas of transparent beating wings
helicopter manoeuvres delight the eye

As summer ended
tiny finches fed on yellow dandelions
others waiting upon fence tops
to flutter down and join the feast

As summer ended
monumental tides rolled in and out
moon waxing larger with each passing night
a half-pearl suspended upon heaven's starry vault

As summer ended
white goshawks soared on gliding wings
seabirds clumped drunkenly on choppy waves
horses ambled, grazing green paddocks

As summer ended
colours, moods and patterns
played out their yearly rituals
and a prayer rose for all the summers yet to come

Thérèse Corfiatis

Bird Haiku

tiny birds flitting
beating heart of the garden
songburst within green

Thérèse Corfiatis

Good Friday Full Moon
19/4/2019

Moon spills supernatural light
upon the earth and sea –
troubles on our planet
Christ consciousness dormant
struggling to awake
where truth seekers, like Julian Assange
hiding from unjust retribution
are dragged from safe refuge
to face condemnation and punishment

Today we remember the man from Galilee
hung upon a cross, for speaking his truth
just as countless souls before and after him
have fallen beneath unforgiving skies –
too many sacrificial lambs
too much sorrow

Tonight, the moon in splendour
reveals its silent truth
huge, round, golden
a plumped-up fertile seed
inseminating our atmosphere
with charged light
impregnating our world with dreams and hope

We, her children of every continent
inhabit a planet round as a womb
revolving a sun, God's golden eye
spinning in never ending cycles
birth, death and rebirth
reminders of the vast unknown
of all we have yet to learn –
a resurrection of true and abiding love

Thérèse Corfiatis

Peach Haiku

sweet scent of peaches
colours of a sunset sky
body and soul fed

Thérèse Corfiatis

Retrospective

Looking back
faded memories
glittering in the trees
defend my covenant

Britta Stenberg

Seagull Variations

Seagulls soar together
wings almost touching tip to tip

the watcher
observes their flight
feathers almost translucent
sunlight shining through them
like a candle's waxen glow

they swerve and swoop as one
as if swimming an upturned sea
then, curve and bend
a history of their passage
patterning a burgeoning blue
like a series of musical notes

movement, sound, vibration
pulse and ripple across the sky
an optical illusion
as they pass overhead

tiny heads shift back and forth
breathing in life and light
breathing out a freedom known only to birds
not to those of us earthbound below

Thérèse Corfiatis

Sing a Song Just for Me

Sing a song for me, I asked
You already have all the songs inside you
he exclaimed

But I can't hear them
in this terrible time
of isolation and misery
I really need them, I cried

Silent tears fell upon my hand
grieving teardrops
with all my doubts

Be with me, I said
I always am, he replied
Every time you fill your thoughts
with poetry
they are my voice singing
he said

Britta Stenberg

Visit to a Nursing Home

for Mavis Hill

I lean forward
listening carefully
her voice is very soft
no inner strength to drive it

her face lights up
its happiness, especially for me
swelling my heart
with a small wave of perfect joy

she rails against the vestiges of age
and gazing on her fragility
I ponder the twists and turns of her long life

and so, the visit creates its own energies
laughter and delight in recollections gathered –
a Durham lass rises up before me
her pale, red hair gleams
a vision of loveliness and youth
sparkling eyes, clear bright skin
her children, grandchildren and great-grandchildren
sprung from her like budding branches
standing quietly in her shadow

and in all her fragility
she shines like a star
nine decades and more
sit proudly on her shoulders
like a queen
enthroned beneath a blossoming tree

Thérèse Corfiatis

www.ingramcontent.com/pod-product-compliance
Lightning Source LLC
Chambersburg PA
CBHW070333120526
44590CB00017B/2861